PRAYERS FOR HEALING

Prayers For Healing

A Nondenominational Collection of Prayers For Those In Crises.

by William H. Hull, M.A.

Biblical quotations herein are from the Holy Bible, New
International Version. Copyright 1973, 1978, 1984
International Bible Society. Used by permission of
Zondervan Bible Publishers and identified on
each page by the initials NIV.

Production by Stanton Publication Services, Minneapolis
Copyright © 1987
William H. Hull
6833 Creston Road
Edina, MN 55435

ISBN # 0-939330-02-4

10 9 8 7 6 5 4 3 2 1

Contents

BOOK FOUR

BOOK FIVE

BOOK SIX

Introduction

I believe that God heals. I don't think it is necessarily in a tent setting because I am too reserved for that, but healing through prayer to God is a very personal act. I do not expect miracles daily because we wouldn't recognize them anyway but I do believe in taking your problems to God for discussion. Providing we can accept His decision which may or may not be the answer we desired. Such help might even be to move the ill person closer to the hereafter and the glorious future which Christians and some others believe exists. I frequently pray with people that we may accept God's decision of our destiny and not to fight it for egoistic reasons.

The need for this book came about when I saw a dear friend die under great pain from cancer. Her husband found it difficult to pray his exact thoughts and came to me for help, pointing out that he could find no books of prayers for healing. I researched the libraries and agreed—there is very little available.

These prayers were assembled by approaching headquarters of ninety-nine different religious groups in the United States, including Christian and non-Christian groups. I'm personally elated to share the prayers from some groups unique to Christians, such as the Antiochian Orthodox Christian Archdiocese of North

America and the Baha'i Faith, along with others. I pray even more will respond before the book goes to press in order that we can exchange prayers to God.

I am asssembling and editing these prayers, not because of some special privilege to do so, but because I see the need and because I have pledged to tithe any future profits herefrom to my own Presbyterian church in a Minneapolis suburb.

Like many people, I was practically dragged to church three times each Sunday before being baptized in the Southern Baptist convention. God rest my beloved mother's soul for that. When I left home to be educated in a Methodist college and later a large Methodist graduate university, my dear mother feared that they would "make a Methodist out of me." They did, too, but it took many years. After our daughters had been confirmed as Methodists, we became restless and spent an entire year attending services at a different church — and denomination — every Sunday. It was a marvelous experience and we highly recommend it — and we found our home in Christ Presbyterian church in Edina, Minnesota.

There we've been very active. I've helped start a Shepherding program, studied for two years to be a Stephen minister and recently became a deacon.

That should be enough background to convince you I'm not too much of a rogue.

William H. Hull

BOOK ONE

Be Merciful To Me, Lord

Be merciful to me, Lord, for I am faint;
  Oh Lord, heal me, for my bones are in agony.
My soul is in anguish.
  How long, O Lord, how long?

Turn, O Lord, and deliver me;
  save me because of your unfailing love.

I am worn out from groaning;
  all night long I flood my bed with weeping
and drench my couch with tears.

My eyes grow weak with sorrow;
  they fail because of all my foes.

Away from me, all you who do evil,
  for the Lord has heard my weeping.
The Lord has heard my cry for mercy;
  the Lord accepts my prayer.

Psalm 6 selections
The Holy Bible (NIV)

A Prayer For One Who Is Sick

O Father of mercies and God of all comfort, our only help in time of need: We humbly beseech you to behold, visit and relieve Your sick servant for whom our prayers are desired.

Look upon him with the eyes of Your mercy; comfort him with the sense of Your goodness; preserve him from the temptations of the enemy; and give him patience under his affliction. In Your good time, restore him to health, and enable him to lead the residue of his life in Your fear, and to Your glory; and grant that finally he may dwell with You in life everlasting; through Jesus Christ our Lord.

Amen.

Frances C. Tindal
The Cathedral Church of St. Paul (Episcopal)
Orlando, Florida

Healing

O God, my God! I beg of thee by the ocean of Thy healing, and by the splendors of the Daystar of Thy Grace, and by Thy Name through which Thou didst subdue Thy servants, and by the pervasive power of Thy most exalted Word and the potency of Thy most august Pen, and by Thy mercy that hath preceded the creation of all who are in heaven and on earth, to purge me with the waters of Thy bounty from every affliction and disorder, and from all weakness and feebleness.

Thou seest, O my Lord, Thy suppliant waiting at the door of Thy bounty, and him who has set his hopes on Thee clinging to the cord of Thy generosity. Deny him not, I beseech Thee, the things he seekest from the ocean of Thy grace and the Daystar of Thy loving kindness.

Powerful art Thou to do what pleaseth Thee. There is none other God save Thee, the Ever-Forgiving, the Most Generous.

From *Baha'i Prayers: A Selection of Prayers Revealed by Baha'u'llah, the Bab, and Abdul-Baha*, copyright by National Spiritual Assembly of the Baha'is of the United States. ISBN #0–87743–175–2. Reproduced by special permission.

Show Me Your Ways, O Lord

Show me your ways, O Lord,
  teach me your paths;
guide me in your truth and teach me,
  for you are God my Savior,
  and remember my hope is in you all day long.
Remember, O Lord, your great mercy and love,
  for they are from of old.
Remember not the sins of my youth
  and my rebellious ways;
according to your love remember me,
  for you are good, O Lord.

Turn to me and be gracious to me,
  for I am lonely and afflicted.
The troubles of my heart have multiplied;
  free me from my anguish.
Look upon my affliction and my distress
  and take away all my sins.
See how my enemies have increased
  and how fiercely they hate me!
Guard my life and rescue me;
  let me not be put to shame,
  for I take refuge in you.

Psalm 25, The Holy Bible (NIV).

I Cry Out Before You

O Lord, the God who saves me,
  day and night I cry out before you.
May my prayer come before you;
  turn your ear to my cry.

For my soul is full of trouble
  and my life draws near the grave.
I am counted among those who go down to the pit;
  I am like a man without strength.
I am set apart with the dead,
  like the slain who lie in the grave,
whom you remember no more,
  who are cut off from your care.

You have put me in the lowest pit,
  in the darkest depths.
Your wrath lies heavily upon me;
  you have overwhelmed me with all your waves.
You have taken from me my closest friends
  and have made me repulsive to them.
I am confined and cannot escape;
  my eyes are dim with grief.

I call to you, O Lord, every day;
  I spread out my hands to you.
Do you show your wonders to the dead?
  Do those who are dead rise up and praise you?
Is your love declared in the grave,
  your faithfulness in Destruction?

Are your wonders known in the place of darkness,
   or your righteous deeds in the land of oblivion?

But I cry to you for help, O Lord;
   in the morning my prayer comes before you.
Why, O Lord, do you reject me
   and hide your face from me?

From my youth I have been afflicted and close to death;
   I have suffered your terrors and am in despair.
Your wrath has swept over me;
   your terrors have destroyed me.
All day long they surround me like a flood;
   they have completely engulfed me.
You have taken my companions and loved ones from
   me;
   the darkness is my closest friend.

Suggested by the "Service Book of the Holy Eastern
Orthodox Catholic and Apostolic Church."
Psalm 88. The Holy Bible (NIV).

Give Attention

Give attention to your servant's prayer and his plea for mercy, O Lord, my God. Hear the cry and the prayer that your servant is praying in your presence this day.

Amen.

Solomon speaking to God. 1 Kings 8:27, The Holy Bible

A Second Prayer

O Lord, my God, who by thy word alone didst heal chronic and temporal diseases; who also didst cure the kinswoman of Peter of her fever. Thou who chastiseth with pity and healeth according to thy goodness, and canst put aside every malady and infirmity: Do thou, the same Lord, now also relieve thy servant, and cure me of the sickness with which I am grieved, and get me up from my bed of pain, sending upon me thy mercy; and grant me health and complete cure. For thou art the Physician of our souls and bodies, and unto thee we ascribe glory: to the Father, and to the Son, and to the Holy Spirit: now and ever, and unto ages of ages. Amen.

Reprinted with permision from the "Service Book of the Holy Eastern Orthodox Catholic and Apostolic Church." However, the editor has changed the prayer from third to first person.

The Jesus Prayer

O Lord Jesus Christ, Son of God, have mercy upon me, a sinner.

(The "Jesus" Prayer may be used at any time, day or night. Also it may be used as basis for mental prayer by repeating it frequently with reverence, and contemplating all of its deep spiritual implications. This prayer is in extensive use by many Monks in the Orthodox-Catholic Church.)

Reprinted with permission from the "Service Book of the Holy Eastern Orthodox Catholic and Apostolic Church."

My Body That Is Sick Unto Death

Dear Father in Heaven: I thank you that you are my Father, because of the Blood of Jesus, your only begotten Son that was shed for my sins. I thank you for that High Priest who has passed through the heavens, and has paid for my redemption with His own life — the just for the unjust. I thank you that in Him I stand complete, justified freely by your grace. I praise you that your Word declares that because of Jesus, I can come boldly unto the throne of grace, that I would obtain mercy, and find grace in time of need.

Lord, in thy presence, I humbly bow, and ask that you search my heart for any unclean thing that is hidden there. As I make confession of my sins, I ask that you turn the searchlight of your Word through your Holy Spirit on my heart, and I will be quick to confess that which is displeasing to you, and in humble reliance on your Holy Spirit to turn from my wicked ways, and to seek your face.

Lord, even as I ask you for healing of my soul from the sins I have committed and their effects, I also ask for physical healing of my body that is sick unto death. I acknowledge my sin before you, and freely admit that my sin was the doorway that this disease took to enter my body. In repentance therefor I call on the Name of the Lord in faith in the sustitutionary of Jesus and reach forth to touch, as it were, the hem of your garment unworthy as I am. But you are worthy, and it is in Your Name, Lord Jesus, as my High Priest, I make this request to Father. I ask for this good gift in order that you may be glorified in my life, and that many may see, and fear, and put their trust in you. I ask in faith, believing that I shall receive, according to Your will, as You see fit. I thank you for hearing me, forgiving me my sins, and for initiating the process of healing both on my soul and my body. Lord, even as You have blessed me, please use me to now go and bless others, to give them the cup of water in Jesus' Name, even as You have let me come to You and drink. Thank you for Your grace . . . and for the help in time of need.

In Jesus' Name, to Whom be all the glory.

Amen.

Charles S.
Presbyterian
Birmingham, AL

Leaving This World Without Fear

Eternal God, we thank you for the gift of life, for your Word. We are children not of this world but of your Eternal Kingdom.

Thank you, O God, _____ believes in you and faces leaving this world without fear, assured in the promise of Jesus Christ (she/he) will live forever in your Eternal Kingdom.

In the name of Jesus Christ I claim for each member of this family your promise — "Blessed are they that mourn, for they shall be comforted."* Bless _____ with the assurance you will care for each member of this family.

Enable each one of us, O God, who remain in this world to witness to your eternal love, with courage through the power of your Holy Spirit.

We claim for our (brother/sister) in Christ, the celebration of the glorious wonder of your Eternal Kingdom, to see you, Jesus Christ, our personal Lord and Savior, face to face, in whose precious name we pray.

Amen

*Matthew 5:4

Roger R. Anderson
Edina, MN

BOOK TWO

Don't Take Me Yet, Lord

Oh, God, don't call me away yet.
I don't want to die.

I know you have prepared a special place for me—
A place I want to see—and to spend eternity.

And, Oh, God, I thank you for that place
And hope I am worthy of being accepted therein.

But, Most Gracious Father,
You have seen fit in your magnanimity
To teach me many lessons—
Lessons which I hope to teach younger people before
I die—
Lessons of love, and caring, and Christian support.
I want to share with them that wisdom you have giv-
en me.

In your great goodness, Oh Lord,
Give me time to do these things.
Give me the wisdom to share with others.
Give me the skills to teach them
Of the great love you have for each of us.

Don't gather me into your eternal flock yet, Oh Lord,
Until I have served you better.

Let me help others
So more of the world can move ahead
Toward the tranquility that comes
With the knowledge of Jesus.

I ask this in the name of your Beloved Son,
Jesus the Christ.

William H. Hull

Breathe on Me, Breath of God

Breathe on me, Breath of God,
    Fill me with life anew
That I may love what Thou dost love,
    And do what Thou wouldst do.

Breathe on me, Breath of God,
    Until my heart is pure,
Until with Thee I will one will,
    To do or to endure.

Breathe on me, Breath of God,
    Till I am wholly Thine,
Till all this earthly part of me
    Glows with Thy fire divine.

Breathe on me, Breath of God,
    So shall I never die;
But live with Thee the perfect life
    Of Thine eternity.

Submitted by *Frances C. Tindal*
by Edwin Hatch.
The Cathedral Church of St. Paul (Episcopal)
Orlando, FLA

No Room In You For Illness

(Christian name), I anoint you with oil in the name of God the Father who created you; in the name of God the Son, Jesus, who died to redeem you; in the name of God the Holy Spirit, who lives within you. And I/we lay my/our hands upon you, beseeching the mercy of our Lord Jesus, that he will so fill you and surround you with his healing light and love and power that there be no room in you for illness, darkness, sin or disease. But penetrating to the depths of your being in mind, body and spirit you will be cleansed, purified, healed, strengthened, renewed and made whole.

Lord, we thank you for hearing our prayer. We know that you always hear our prayer. So, we thank you for the healing power already at work in this your servant. Continue that good work which you have begun in him/her. Raise him/her up. Make him/her strong. Send him/her on his/her way rejoicing, praising your holy name, enabled to share that gift which you have given him/her.

And the blessing of God Almighty, Father, Son, and Holy Spirit, be upon you and give you peace, this day and always.

Amen.

Donald E. Baustian
Christ Episcopal Church
Little Rock, AR

The Prayer Of The Chalice

Father, to Thee I raise my whole being,
. . . a vessel emptied of self. Accept, Lord
this my emptiness, and so fill me with
Thyself—Thy Light, Thy Love, Thy
Life—that these Thy precious Gifts
may radiate through me and over-
flow the chalice of my heart into
the hearts of all with whom I
come in contact this day
revealing unto them
the beauty of
Thy Joy
and
Whole-
ness
and
the
serenity
of Thy Peace
which nothing can destroy.

St. Luke's Press, Richmond, VA. Used by special permission.

Your Faith Has Healed You

A woman was there who had been subject to bleeding for twelve years, but no one could heal her. She came up behind Jesus and touched the edge of his cloak and immediately her bleeding stopped.

When Jesus asked who had touched him, Peter exclaimed that the crowd was large but Jesus insisted that "Someone touched me; I know that power has gone out from me."

Then the woman, seeing that she could not go unnoticed, came trembling and fell at his feet. In the presence of all the people, she told why she had touched him and how she had been instantly healed. Then he said to her, "Daughter, your faith has healed you. Go in peace."

While Jesus was still speaking, a messenger came from the house of Jairus, the synagogue ruler, to tell him that Jairus' daughter was dead. Jesus said to Jairus "Don't be afraid; just believe and she will be healed." At the house of Jairus, Jesus did indeed raise the daughter from the dead.

Luke 8 selections
The Holy Bible (NIV)

Prayer Of A Sick Person

O Lord Jesus Christ, our Saviour, the Physician of souls and bodies, who didst become man and suffered death on the cross for our salvation, and through thy tender love and compassion didst heal all manner of sickness and affliction: do thou O Lord, visit me in my suffering, and grant me grace and strength to bear this sickness with which I am afflicted, with Christian patience and submission to thy will, trusting in thy loving kindness and tender mercy. Bless, I pray thee, the means used for my recovery, and those who administer them. I know O Lord, that I justly deserve any punishment thou mayest inflict upon me, for I have so often offended thee and sinned against thee, in thought, word, and deed. Therefore, I humbly pray thee, look upon my weakness, and deal not with me after my sins, but according to the multitude of thy mercies. Have compassion on me, and let mercy and justice meet and deliver me from this sickness and suffering I am undergoing. Grant that my sickness may be the means of my true repentance and amendment of my life according to thy will, that I may spend the rest of my days in thy love and fear; that my soul, being helped by thy grace and sanctified by thy Holy Mysteries, may be prepared for its passage to the Eternal Life. And there, in the company of thy blessed Saints, may praise and glorify thee with thy Eternal Father and Life-giving Spirit. Amen.

Reprinted with permission from the "Service Book of the Holy Eastern Orthodox Catholic and Apostolic Church."

Commanding Light

We thank you for commanding light to shine out of darkness, for stretching out the heavens, and laying the foundations of the earth; for making all things through your Word. We thank you for creating us in your image and for calling us to be your people, for revealing your purpose in the law and the prophets, and for dealing patiently with our pride and disobedience.

Mother-Father-Christ

Let me now be filled with thy loving, healing light.

Let the light of life flood into me,
   filling me completely
   with radiant, beautiful light, now.

Let any part of my body where there may be dis-ease
   or darkness
   be filled with your loving, healing light.

Let any blocks or obstructions to healing,
   to receiving,
   be gently washed away.

Let me *see* every cell of my body
   filled with your loving, healing light.

Let me see that light anchoring into each cell.

Let me *know* now and accept now
   that every cell of my being,
   every cell of my body,
   is completely, fully and totally alive.

Let me see now that there is no limit
   to the amount of light, love and healing
   I may receive;

I open myself completely to receiving that now.

Let me continue to receive this eternal,
  never-ending stream of light and love
  now and forever, so be it.

Amen

Pauline Conn
Minneapolis, MN

Prayer In Time Of Trouble

Oh, God, our help and assistance, who art just and merciful, and who heareth the supplications of thy people; look down upon me, a miserable sinner, have mercy upon me, and deliver me from this trouble that besets me, for which I know, I am deservedly suffering. I acknowledge and believe, O Lord, that all trials of this life are given by Thee for our chastisement, when we drift away from thee, and disobey, thy commandments; deal not with me after my sins, but according to thy bountiful mercies, for I am the work of Thy hands, and thou knowest my weakness. Grant me, I beseech thee, thy divine helping grace, and endow me with patience and strength to endure my tribulations with complete submission to Thy Will. Thou knowest my misery and suffering and to Thee, my only hope and refuge, I flee for relief and comfort; trusting to thine infinite love and compassion, that in due time, when thou knowest best, thou wilt deliver me from this trouble and turn my distress into comfort, when I shall rejoice in thy mercy, and exalt and praise thy Holy Name, O Father, Son, and Holy Spirit: now and ever, and unto ages of ages. Amen.

Reprinted with permission from the "Service Book of the Holy Eastern Orthodox Catholic and Apostolic Church."

Whom Shall I Fear?

The Lord is my light and my salvation —
  whom shall I fear?

One thing I ask of the Lord,
  this is what I seek:
that I may dwell in the house of the Lord
  all the days of my life.
to gaze upon the beauty of the Lord
  and to seek him in his temple.
For in the day of trouble
  he will keep me safe in his dwelling;
he will hide me in the shelter of his tabernacle
  and set me high upon a rock.

Hear my voice when I call, O Lord;
  be merciful to me and answer me.
My heart says of you, "Seek his face!"
  Your face, Lord, I will seek.
Do not hide your face from me,
  do not turn your servant away in anger;
  you have been my helper.
Do not reject me or forsake me,
  O God my Savior.

Teach me your way, O Lord;
  lead me in a straight path.

I am still confident of this:
  I will see the goodness of the Lord
  in the land of the living.

Be strong and take heart
and wait for the Lord.

Psalm 27. The Holy Bible (NIV)

BOOK THREE

He Will Not Always Accuse

The Lord is compassionate and gracious,
  slow to anger, abounding in love.
He will not always accuse,
  not will he harbor his anger forever;
he does not treat us as our sins deserve
  or repay us according to our iniquities.
For as high as the heavens are above the earth,
  so great is his love for those who fear him;
as far as the east is from the west,
  so far has he removed our transgressions from us.
As a father has compassion on his children,
  so the Lord has compassion on those who fear him;
for he knows how we are formed,
  he remembers that we are dust.
As for man, his days are like grass,
  he flourishes like a flower of the field;
the wind blows over it and it is gone,
  and its place remembers it no more.
But from everlasting to everlasting
  the Lord's love is with those who fear him,
  and his righteousness with their children's
  children —

with those who keep his covenant
  and remember to obey his precepts.

The Lord has established his throne in heaven,
   and his kingdom rules over all.

Praise the Lord, O my soul.

Psalm 103. The Holy Bible (NIV)

Feed My Sheep

Shepherd, show me how to go
  O'er the hillside steep,
How to gather, how to sow, —
  How to feed Thy sheep;
I will listen for Thy voice,
  Lest my footsteps stray;
I will follow and rejoice
  All the rugged way.

Thou wilt bind the stubborn will,
  Wound the callous breast,
Make self-righteousness be still,
  Break earth's stupid rest.
Strangers on a barren shore,
  Lab'ring long and lone,
We would enter by the door,
  And Thou know'st Thine own.

So, when day grows dark and cold,
  Tear or triumph harms,
Lead Thy lambkins to the fold,
  Take them in Thine arms;
Feed the hungry, heal the heart,
  Till the morning's beam;
White as wool ere they depart,
  Shepherd, wash them clean.

Mary Baker Eddy
"Miscellaneous Writings"
In public domain.

The Righteous Will Live By Faith

I am not ashamed of the gospel, because it is the power of God for the salvation of everyone who believes: first for the Jew, then for the Gentile. For in the gospel a righteousness from God is revealed, a righteousness that is by faith from first to last, just as it is written: "The righteous will live by faith."

Romans 1. The Holy Bible (NIV).
As delivered by the Rev. Dr. Roger Anderson in a sermon at Christ Presbyterian Church, Edina, MN, December 21, 1986.

I Fade Away Like An Evening Shadow

O Sovereign Lord,
　deal well with me for your name's sake;
　out of the goodness of your heart deliver me.

For I am poor and needy,
　and my heart is wounded within me.
I fade away like an evening shadow;
　I am shaken off like a locust.

My knees give way from fasting:
　my body is thin and gaunt.
I am an object of scorn to my accusers;
　when they see me, they shake their heads.

Help me, O Lord, my God;
　save me in accordance with your love.
With my mouth I will greatly extol the Lord;
　in the great throng I will praise him.
For he stands at the right hand of the needy one,
　to save his life from those who condemn him.

Psalm 109 selections
The Holy Bible (NIV)

A Prayer For Time

Dear God,

You have my life in your control,
  as I have said before.
I place my life, my being, my future
  in your hands for eternity.

But, Oh, Lord, I am in dire circumstances now;
  I need your attentive love.
I need your succor and pray for it.
  But whatever must be, must be . . .
And I do accept your decisions for the remainder
  of my earthly life.

But, dear God, can't you please
  extend my stay on earth?
That I might do more to honor your name
  and that of your son, Jesus Christ.

Only recently have I truly learned how great
  it is to serve you,
How much my work is needed to help my fellow man
  in your holy name.

Please, God, let this pestilence be removed from me.
  Give me sufficient health and strength
To continue in your name.
  Let me serve you on earth a while longer.

But, Oh, lord, if you cannot grant my plea
   then do with me as you will.
And when you decide to send for me
   to bring me to life eternal,
Grant that my passing will be quick and silent
   As easy on my beloved ones as is possible
As is the passing of the least of all your children.

I pray these things in your son's name.
   Amen.

William H. Hull

The Fountain Of Life

Oh Lord you preserve both man and beast
  How priceless is your unfailing love!
Both high and low among men
  find refuge in the shadow of your wings.
They feast on the abundance of your house;
  you give them drink from your river of delights.
For with you is the fountain of life;
  in your light we see light.

Continue your love to those who know you,
  your righteousness to the upright in heart.

Psalm 36. The Holy Bible (NIV)

You Can Be Healed

The first requirement for healing is faith. If there is doubt and unbelief in your mind that God will not do what He has promised in His Word, you will receive nothing from Him. When our faith actually makes contact with God, we suddenly receive a full assurance that God has heard our prayers and He will do that thing asked for.

Sometimes God tries our faith to see how strong it is by delaying the answer. When he finds that our trust is completely in Him and His power to heal, the answer comes! Regardless of your case, how hopeless it may seem, our God is able to make you completely well and strong! God delights in doing the impossible for those who will step out in faith and believe Him.

William H. Carey
National Gay Pentecostal Alliance
Schenectady, NY
Copyrighted by Search for Truth Publications,
Inc., Houston, TX. Used by special permission.

But Christ Has Indeed
Been Raised . . .

But if it is preached that Christ has been raised from the dead, how can some of you say that there is no resurrection of the dead? If there is no resurrection of the dead, then not even Christ has been raised. And if Christ has not been raised, our preaching is useless and so is your faith. More than that, we are then found to be false witnesses about God, for we have testified about God that he raised Christ from the dead. But he did not raise him if in fact the dead are not raised. For if the dead are not raised, then Christ has not been raised either. And if Christ has not ben raised, your faith is futile; you are still in your sins. Then those also who have fallen asleep in Christ are lost. If only for this life we have hope in Christ, we are to be pitied, more than all men.

But *Christ has indeed been raised from the dead!*

Paul writing to the Corinthians—1 Corinthians 15:12–19. The Holy Bible (NIV)

I Cry Out By Day

My God, My God, why have you forsaken me?
  Why are you so far from saving me,
  so far from the words of my groaning?
O my God, I cry out by day but you do not answer,
  by night, and am not silent.

Yet you are enthroned as the Holy One;
  you are the praise of Israel.
In you our fathers put their trust;
  they trusted and you delivered them.
They cried to you and were saved;
  in you they trusted and were not disappointed.

But I am a worm and not a man,
  scorned by men and despised by the people.
All who see me mock me;
  they hurl insults, shaking their heads:
"He trusts in the Lord;
  let the Lord rescue him.

Let him deliver him,
  since he delights in him."

Yet you brought me out of the womb;
  you made me trust in you
  even at my mother's breast.
From birth I was cast upon you;
  from my mother's womb you have been my God.

Do not be far from me,
   for trouble is near
   and there is no one to help.

But you, O Lord, be not far off;
   O my Strength, come quickly to help me.
I will declare your name to my brothers;
   in the congregation I will praise you.
You who fear the Lord, praise him!
   All you descendants of Jacob, honor him!
   Revere him, all you descendants of Israel!

From you comes my praise in the great assembly;
   before those who fear you will I fulfill my vows.
The poor will eat and be satisfied;
   they who seek the Lord will praise him—
   may your hearts live forever!
All the ends of the earth
   will remember and turn to the Lord,
and all the families of the nations
   will bow down before him.

Psalm 22. The Holy Bible (NIV)

Because He Lives

O God our Father, creator of the world and giver of all good things: we thank you for our home on earth and for the joy of living. We praise you for your love in Jesus Christ, who came to set things right, who died rejected on the cross and rose triumphant from the dead. Because he lives, we live to praise you, Father, Son and Holy Spirit, our God forever.

BOOK FOUR

Evening Prayer

Eternal God: you gave your Son Jesus to be light of the world. In his light, help us to face our darkness, to confess our sins, and, trusting your mercy, to rest in peace this night, so that with the coming of the day we may wake in good faith to serve you; through Jesus Christ our Lord. Amen.

God our Father: in Jesus Christ you called us to come when we are weary and overburdened. Give us rest from the trials of the day; guard our sleep and speak to our dreaming, so that refreshed we may greet daylight with resolve, and be strong to do your will; through Jesus Christ our Lord. Amen.

He Lives In Us

We are already children of God. His commandments are these: that we believe in his Son Jesus Christ, and that we love one another. Whoever keeps his commandments lives in God and God lives in him. We know he lives in us by the Spirit he has given us.

Is Any One Of You In Trouble?

Is any one of you in trouble? He should pray. Is anyone happy? Let him sing songs of praise. Is any one of you sick? He should call the elders of the church to pray over him and anoint him with oil in the name of the Lord. And the prayer offered in faith will make the sick person well; the Lord will raise him up. If he has sinned, he will be forgiven. (James 5:13–15)

We have an ordinance in the church identified as "administration to the sick" . . . in response to the scriptural admonition as found (in the quotation above) and is provided to ask for divine help toward the healing of the recipient.

Generally, two elders participate. One anoints with oil while pronouncing a spontaneous prayer, acknowledgding the act and its purpose; admonishing for faith and courage; and emphasizing the assurance of the sufficiency of God for all human needs. The second elder offers a prayer of confirmation addressed to God in gratitude, while acknowledging dependence upon Him for spiritual, mental and physical blessings. In accordance with the scriptural admonition referred to, such a prayer will often relate to an affirmation of faith, praise to our Lord, ask for forgiveness of trespasses, and request divine intervention and guidance for the days ahead. In each case, the prayer is spontaneous as the elder involved feels inclined and so led.

Aleah Koury
Reorganized Church of Jesus Christ of Latter Day Saints
Independence, MO

Also submitted by
Jim Stevens
Belden, MS

A Living Hope

Praise be to the God and Father of our Lord Jesus Christ! In his great mercy he has given us new birth into a living hope through the resurrection of Jesus Christ from the dead, and into an inheritance that can never perish, spoil or fade — kept in heaven for you, who through faith are shielded by God's power until the coming of the salvation that is ready to be revealed in the last time. In this you greatly rejoice, though now for a little while you may have had to suffer grief in all kinds of trials.

These have come so that your faith — of greater worth than gold, which perishes even though refined by fire — may be proved genuine and may result in praise, glory and honor when Jesus Christ is revealed. Though you have not seen him, you love him; and even though you do not see him now, you believe him and are filled with an inexpressible and glorious joy, for you are receiving the goal of your faith, the salvation of your souls.

1 Peter 1:3–9. The Holy Bible (NIV)

We Give Ourselves To You

O, God, who called us from death to life: we give ourselves to you; and with the church through all ages, we thank you for your saving love in Jesus Christ our Lord.

Responding To The Lord

I could never pay back what the Lord has given me. Like the person who works hard doing the Lord's work, "not for building up my chances to get into Heaven, but to respond to what the Lord has given me."

Dr. Boswell J. Clark
The Kirk of the Keys (Presbyterian)
Marathon, FLA

My Heart Yearns For Him

*(Job's conclusion after a long, pessimistic disser-
tation.)*

He has alienated my brothers from me;
   my acquaintances are completely estranged from
   me.

My kinsmen have gone away;
   my friends have forgotten me.
My guests and maidservants count me as a stranger;
   They look upon me as an alien.
I summon my servant, but he does not answer
   though I beg him with my own mouth.
My breath is offensive to my wife;
   I am loathsome to my own brothers.
Even the little boys scorn me;
   when I appear, they ridicule me.
All my intimate friends detest me;
   Those I love have turned against me.
I am nothing but skin and bones;
   I have escaped with only the skin of my teeth.

I know that my Redeemer lives,
   and that in the end he will stand upon the earth.
And after my skin has been destroyed
   yet in my flesh I shall see God;
I myself will see him
   with my own eyes—I, and not another.
How my heart yearns within me!

Job 19:13–27, The Holy Bible (NIV)

Heaven

I've thought of life hereafter
And wonder if it's true
If there is love and laughter
And sunbeams shining through.
St. Peter at the Pearly Gates
While Gabriel blows his horn.
And if they make the people wait
So each can take his turn
To enter through one by one —
Or is it two by two?
And do you meet new friends
Or find the ones you knew?
Is it really beautiful
Or is it a state of mind?
Are the angels really winged
Or are they the special kind?
Are the stairs made of gold
Or is that, too, a dream?
Wouldn't it be nice to know
That all there is serene?

Gerry Swanson
Trinity Lutheran Church
Minneapolis, MN

A Prayer For Healing

Blessed Father: Draw near to us now as we draw near to you. This body is torn with pain, which brings sweat to the brow, torment to the mind, and grieving to the heart. Our Lord understands that, Father. He suffered more than any man and He did it for us.

Help us now to reach out by faith and receive the healing touch of the One by whose stripes we are healed. Grant, we pray, an easing of the pain, a mending of the tissues, a recovering of strength, a peace to the heart and a renewing of faith.

We worship and praise you, O loving heavenly Father, through our Lord and Savior Jesus.

Amen.

A. Graybill Brubaker
Brethren in Christ Church
Chambersburg, PA

Raise Us To New Life

Eternal Father, guardian of our lives: we confess that we are children of dust, unworthy of your gracious care. We have not loved as we ought to love, nor have we lived as you command, and our years are soon gone. Lord God, have mercy on us. Forgive our sin and raise us to new life, so that as long as we live we may serve you, until, dying, we enter the joy of your presence; through Jesus Christ our Lord.

Amen.

From *The Worshipbook – Services*. Copyright © MCMLXX The Westminster Press. Used by permission.

BOOK FIVE

The Sermon

I sat in church and listened
    the words he spoke to all
And yet, it seemed to me
    He had listened to my call.
A plea for understanding
    to find the way back home.
A life that's so demanding
    I can't do it all alone.
He said "God will show the way."
    that's all I really ask
But finding it by myself
    I've found is quite a task.
The people bowed their heads in prayer.
    Well, I have done that too.
But what I've asked is never there
    So then I pray anew.
Burdens I have many
    But they're not mine alone
My life is quite uncanny
    so much grief I have known.
I know we all must bear a cross
    that's what the Bible says.
But to take continuous loss
    It just does not make sense.
The Golden Rule I've lived by
    almost my whole life
But all I've reaped is sorrow
    and I've had my share of strife.
The more I do for others
    the more I'm turned upon

And if I had my druthers
　　I'd go my way alone.
But I am not made that way
　　I care too much you see;
I love with my whole being
　　those who don't love me.
So, if I'm to find the peace I seek
　　no matter where I go
I will not turn the other cheek.
　　I'll just have to answer "No."
For that has been my problem
　　For others I've been there
But when I look for help I need
　　there is no one to care.
I'll just keep on praying
　　and maybe I'll be heard
And when I am "Look out world!"
　　I'll be freer than a bird.

Gerry Swanson
Trinity Lutheran church
Minneapolis, MN

The Eternal Spring

Today I saw the first daffodil.

The robin
     in his enthusiasm
     burst the vowels with mad song.

The grass turns green
     a blade at a time
While the tree leaves burst their pods
     and the sun warms the soil.

There can be no God before You
     because none could perform
       such miracles
Yet, Lord, some of your chosen ones
     need those miracles too.

Can you shine that glorious warmth on me
     that I, too, can warm and bloom?
Can you help me burst into robin's song
     from sheer inner joy?
Can you let me shed the coating
     of this malady that drags me down
just as the elm does prior to leafing?

In Your infinite mercy,
   In your great and forgiving love
Help me overcome this situation
   into which I am thrust
So I may live to glorify your name.

Amen.

William H. Hull

Thanks For The Gift Of Life

O God, before whom generations rise and pass away: we praise you for all your servants who, having lived this life in faith, now live eternally with you. Especially we thank you for your servant _____, for the gift of his (her) life, for the grace you have given him (her), for all in him (her) that was good and kind and faithful. We thank you that for him (her) death is probably approaching, and pain is ending and he (she) is about to enter the joy you have prepared; through Jesus Christ, our Lord.

Amen.

Down In The Valley

As I was down in the valley
      I looked to the mountain top;
I prayed to the Lord:
      Oh, Lord, please help me. Don't ever stop.

When things are not easy in your life
      You are not to give up, you see.
That's when Jesus can do His work
      In you and in me.

When we're in the valley low
      Is when we have time to grow.
We don't understand why,
      But, believe me, on Jesus we must rely.

So as I get near to the mountain top again,
      I thank you, Jesus, for being my special
      friend.

I'm your child—this is very true.
      Thank you, Jesus, for being with me
In everything I've been through.

S. Phyllis Aspen
Baptist
Montrose, MN

The Great Physician

Lord, you are the Great Physician, the Performer of Miracles, yesterday and always. You know my illness. If it pleases you, send me patience, comfort and rest. Make me grateful for the privilege of suffering pain, so that I may better understand your suffering and pain on the way to the cross, and the gift of salvation when we shall meet face to face. All this and whatever else you see I need, grant me, in Jesus' name.

Amen.

Alice Bakke
Lutheran
Olivia, MN

Prayer For Those Who Are Ill

Merciful Father, we come to You with the petition that You would look with favor upon all those who are ill. Hold them up and support them on Your arms of love as they endure the sufferings, trials and hardships of this present life. Let them remember that only You can really lighten the burdens they bear. Give them the grace to set aside their worrisome thoughts and confidentially to trust in You. Let them never be ashamed of their hope grounded in Your promise that all things will work together for good to those who love you. Restore them in strength and health according to Your good pleasure; in Jesus' name.

Amen.

Alice Bakke
Lutheran
Olivia, MN

He's Always There

I've been ill so many times
  and often wondered why?
But through it all I always knew
  that He was standing by.
I've had parts removed within
  but never was there fear
Because I felt His presence
  and knew that He was near.
My prayers were always answered
  no matter what they were.
If it were loneliness or fear
  I knew that He was there.
So many times I called on him
  while lying in my bed at night
To look down on my friends and kin
  and send His guiding light.
I knew He always heard me
  things worked out just fine.
And knowing that
  surely did give me peace of mind.

Gerry Swanson
Trinity Lutheran Church
Minneapolis, MN

I Am But A Poor Creature

Praise thee Thou, O Lord my God! I implore Thee, Thy Most Great Name through which Thou didst stir up Thy servant and build up Thy city, and Thy most excellent titles, and Thy most august attributes, to assist Thy people to turn in the direction of Thy manifold bounties, and set their faces toward the Tabernacle of Thy wisdom. Heal Thou the sicknesses that have assailed the soul on every side, and have deterred them from directing their gaze toward the Paradise that lieth in the shelter of Thy shadowing Name, which Thou didst ordain to be the King of all names of all who are in heaven and all who are on earth. Potent art Thou to do as pleases Thee. In Thy hands is the empire of all names. There is none other God but Thee, the Mighty, the Wise.

I am but a poor creature, O my Lord; I have clung to the hem of Thy riches. I am sore sick; I have held fast the cord of Thy healing. Deliver me from the ills that have encircled me, and wash me thoroughly with the waters of Thy graciousness and mercy, and attire me with raiment of wholesomeness, through Thy forgiveness and bounty. Fix, then, mine eyes upon Thee, and rid me of all attachment of aught else except Thyself. Aid me to do what Thou desirest, and to fulfill what Thou pleaseth.

Thou are truly the Lord of this life and of the next. Thou art, in truth, the Ever-Forgiving, the Most Merciful.

From *Bah'ai Prayers: A Selection of Prayers Revealed by Baha'u'llah, the Bab, and Abdul-Baha*. Copyright by National Spiritual Assembly of the Baha'is of the United States. ISBN #0–87743–175–2. Reproduced by special permission.

Let Me See The Way Clearly

I glorify you, Oh Lord,
>   Great and wonderful Jesus, I know you.
I praise you to the heavens;
>   I acknowledge your Loving Self.

I cannot deny you.
>   I would not denigrate you.
for you are the world and the after-world.
>   It is you to whom I go when I die;
It is you who went ahead of me
>   to prepare the place.

Take me, Lord, when you need me.
>   use me on this earth
>   or in heaven
wherever I can best serve and glorify you.

If you wish to leave me on earth
>   let me see the way clearly
that I may extend your word—your message.
>   whether it be caring for the ill,
alleviating fears of the worried,
>   feeding the hungry or bathing the soiled,
I am ready, Lord,
>   needing only your direction.

Amen.

William H. Hull

Listen

When I ask you to listen to me and you start giving advice, you have not done what I asked.

When I ask you to listen to me and you begin to tell me why I shouldn't feel that way, you are trampling on my feelings.

When I ask you to listen to me and you feel you have to do something to solve my problems, you have failed me, strange as that may seem.

Listen! All I asked was that you listen. No talk or do. Just hear me.

Advice is cheap. A quarter will get you both Dear Abby and Billy Graham in the same newspaper.

And I can do for myself; I'm not helpless. Maybe discouraged and faltering but not helpless.

When you can do something for me that I can and need to do for myself, you contribute to my fear and weakness.

But when you accept as a simple fact that I feel, no matter how irrational, then I can quit trying to convince you and you can get about the business of understanding what's behind this irrational feeling.

And when that's clear, the answers are obvious and I don't need advice.

Irrational feelings make sense when we understand what's behind them.

Perhaps that's why prayer works . . . because God is mute and He doesn't try to give advice or try to fix things.

So please listen and just hear me. And if you want to talk, wait a minute for your turn; and I'll listen to you.

Author unknown.
Apparently in public domain.

BOOK SIX

With Humility

With humility
    I come before you, my Lord.
I pray that you will consider my pain
    and grant me relief from it.
That you will shine upon me
    the glorious radiance of your Self
In order that I may be reborn
    rejuvenated to your service.
I am so alone
    oh, God!
The trees have their leaves
    the grass has its blades
    the flowers have their blossoms
But me—Oh—God
    I have nothing.
For my head I need a pillow
    For my body I need nourishment.
For my soul I have you
    and I need nothing more.
I shall live, oh, Lord.
    You promised me a better world.
I anticipate it—desire it
    yet here I remain, an outcast
    a lonely soul—without friends
    without courage.

I know you are there, my Father
    I know you care for and watch me

But, Oh, God, forgive me
    For I am but a mere mortal . . .
Worried, concerned, bewildered—
    knowing not where I go from here.
Will you have me minister to others?
    Help the crippled and the ill?
    Feed the hungry?
But I can't, Oh, Lord
    until you remove this illness
    that dominates my life.
Remove it, Lord!
    Banish it!
    Cure me!
Give me revitalized life
    that I may serve you
    as we both wish.
Give me strength, Sweet Jesus,
    to do as you would have me do.

In your name I ask it.
Amen

William H. Hull

Prayer to St. Michael

Saint Michael, the Archangel, defend us in battle; be our defense against the wickedness and snares of the devil. May God rebuke him, we humbly pray; and do you, O Prince of the heavenly host, by the power of God, thrust into hell Satan and the other evil spirits who prowl about the world for the ruin of souls.

Amen

Elizabeth Schreiner
Lakeville, MN

Forgive My Sins, Lord

Dear Lord,

I thank you and praise you for all the blessings
   you have given to me.

Lord, you know about by back problems, my surgery
   and my recent fall
   which has aggravated the pain in my back.

I ask you, Lord, in all humility, to forgive my sins
   and to heal my back

I ask it in the precious name of Jesus
   and I thank you
   and praise you for this healing.

Amen

Doris M. Hansen
St. Louis Park, MN

Lord, Clear Our Vision

Lord, clear our vision lest we perish,
    Lose life and hope and all we cherish.
Open our hearts, our minds, our eyes.
    Lord, with your wisdom, make us wise:
    Say but the word that we may see—
    Lord, heal us all—heal me.

Lord, heal our eyes lest we pass by
    And leave the wounded lone to die;
Lest blind lead blind and fall at night.
    Lord be our guide, Lord, be our light.
    Say but the word that we may see—
    Lord, heal us all—heal me.

Lord, heal us lest our hearts be blind.
    Lord, be our light, heal dark of mind.
Open our thought to know your grace
    And see you in our neighbor's face.
    Say but the word that we may see—
    Lord, heal us all—heal me.

Lord, heal our tongues that we may tell
    The wonders you have done so well;
Lord, heal our will that we may do
    Your service in the love of you.
    Your glory show, your glory see—
    Lord, heal us all—heal me.

Betsy Curtis
Saegertown, PA
(In the public domain.)

We Know From The Word

We know from the Word, O Lord,
that they brought "all the sick" . . .
and that "You healed them" (Matthew 4:24)
We ask You now to heal your servant (their name)
In Christ's name, we pray.
Amen.

Anonymous
Oklahoma City, OK

Let The Signs of My Illness
Drop Away

I am overwhelmed, God
  by my inability to fight the crises
  of my life.
I find the accumulation
  of my many problems and illnesses
  almost more than I can bear.
Yet, God, I know you are with me
  and that you will assist me.
I do pray that, in your great beneficence,
  you will show me the route
  the way I must take
  to conquer these problems.
Oh, God, I pray to you
  I supplicate to you,
  that the way may be very obvious to me.
I am but a poor human being
  made in your image
  but without your ability
  your knowledge, your insight.
I am but a poor copy
  of the Great One, You, oh Lord.
Show me again, Dear Lord
  reveal to me the Great Truths
  show me the open door
  through which I can pass
  to join you forever.
Help me, if it be your choice,
  to fight off this current plague
  that I may live to honor you.

Oh, God, it is so frustrating
  so painful
  when I only want to serve you—
  to help my fellow beings.
I pray that you will give me this opportunity

  this great time—
  to be thy humble servant.

Let the signs of my illness drop away
Let the fevers of my near death disappear
Let the aches of my ravaged body be alienated.

I ask this in the name of your Glorious Son
Jesus.

Forever and forever.

Amen.

William H. Hull

Anyway

People are unreasonable, illogical and self centered,
    Love them anyway.

If you do good, people will accuse you of selfish,
    ulterior motives.
    Do good anyway.

If you are successful, you will win false friends and
    true enemies.
    Succeed anyway.

Honesty and frankness make you vulnerable.
    Be honest and frank anyway.

The good you do today will be forgotten tomorrow.
    Do good anyway.

The biggest people with the biggest ideas can be shot
    down by the smallest people with the smallest
    minds.
    Think big anyway.

People favor underdogs but follow only top dogs.
    Fight for some underdogs anyway.

What you spend years building may be destroyed
    overnight.
    Build anyway.

Give the world the best you have and you'll get kicked
in the teeth.

Give the world the best you have anyway.

Karen Kaiser Clark
St. Paul, MN

A Nurse Speaks Out

I am a nurse and very often a night nurse in home care situations.

I am alone with my patient and troubling circumstances arise. I can always use Psalm 121 as a wonderful prayer:

> "I will lift up mine eyes unto the hills,
> from whence cometh my help.
> My help cometh from the Lord
> which made heaven and earth.
> He will not suffer thy foot to be moved
> He that keepeth thee will not slumber.
> Behold! He that keepeth Israel
> shall neither slumber nor sleep."

This takes away the aloneness and gives me strength and wisdom.

Another favorite and useful prayer is the Lord's Prayer, which I go through especially with the very ill patient.

We start by grabbing our fingers and using one word per finger. Thus "The" (Thumb) "Lord" (1st finger), "is" (2nd finger), "my" (3rd finger), etc. Then I tell my patient to hold on to that fact that the Lord is his/hers and I recite the remainder of the prayer to them. This is very comforting to many adults and to children, who need something tangible to hold onto in their suffering.

Elaine R. Mathiason, R. N.
Christ Presbyterian Church
Edina, MN

The Un-Christmas Card

I cannot wish you a MERRY CHRISTMAS
    When you feel so alone
. . . but I can wish you moments of Peace.
I cannot wish you a JOYOUS SEASON
    When each day brings more tears
. . . but I can wish you moments of HOPE.
I can pray with you that one day
    You will not feel so broken, so fragile
      so fearful
      so "jerked around" by FATE
. . . and I will be there to rejoice with you then
as I am with you now while we wait.

Linda Mahoney
Burnsville, MN
© 1985 Linda Mahoney

I Said A Prayer For You Today

I said a prayer for you today
And know God must have heard.

I felt the answer in my heart
Although He spoke no word.

I didn't ask for wealth or fame
(I knew you wouldn't mind).

I asked Him to send treasures
Of a far more lasting kind.

I asked that He'd be near you
At the start of each new day.

To grant you health and blessings
And friends to share your way.

I asked for happiness for you
In all things great and small.

But it was for His loving care
I prayed the most of all.

Submitted by
Mel Anderson, Minneapolis, MN
and
D. Kodidek, Pomona, NY

Apparently in public domain.

BOOK SEVEN

Thank You for Courage, Lord

Thank you, Dear God, for sending us your Son, who gave us the promise of eternal life. Thank you for the many blessings you have bestowed upon us. Thank you for Love. Thank you for fellow human beings who love — and appreciate — and care for us.

Thank you for the next generation — for children. Thank you for giving us the patience to understand their attempts at independence. Thank you for their eventual awakening.

Thank you for giving us the courage to live from day to day — when many times it is painful and difficult. Give us the strength we need—just to exist at times — to continue serving you. Sometimes it is hard just to live, looking forward to the Great Hereafter.

It is often difficult, Lord, to be the Christian we want to be, to be the Christian you would have us be — to follow the teachings of your Son. Please give us the patience, Lord, the wisdom which we as mere mortals possess in only small degrees compared to your unlimited comprehension. Teach us humility. Teach us love for each other. Teach us respect for individual rights.

And thank you, Lord, for continuing to place your caring hands, and benevolent eyes, upon those of us who are lonely, or tired, or ill.

We love you.

Amen.

William H. Hull

For A Sick Child

Lord Jesus Christ, Good Shepherd of the sheep. You gather the lambs in your arms and carry them in your bosom. We commend to your loving care this child. Relieve his pain, guard him from all danger. Restore to him your gifts of gladness and strength, and raise him up to a life of service to you. Hear us, we pray, for your dear Son's sake.

Rita Montenegro
Chicago, IL

O God Whose Blessed Son

O God, whose blessed Son
did hang upon the shameful Cross,
and for our sakes suffered bitter pain:
Give to us, we pray Thee,
the strength to bear our hurts.
In fever, let Thy peace come upon us;
In anguish, may Thy strength sustain us;
and in all pain
let our eyes dwell upon Thy Son,
that we may behold Thy goodness
and follow Thy way in patience
and in confidence.
More we cannot ask;
with less we cannot live.
Amen.

"I composed this prayer especially for a girl who was
very ill and in great pain. I did not know her very
well but was concerned about her. One night about 3
A.M. I woke up—and knew she was going to be
alright. I do not remember having that experience
before."

William H. Crouch
Retired Episcopal Rector
Concord, New Hampshire

This Is Another Day

This is another day. I know what it will bring forth,
  but make me ready, Lord, for whatever it may be.
If I am to stand up, help me to stand bravely.
If I am to sit still, help me to sit quietly.
If I am to lie low, help me to do it patiently.
And if I am to do nothing, let me do it gallantly.
Make these words more than words, and give me the
  Spirit of Jesus.

When I begin to feel better, Lord, let me not forget
  Thee.
If I turn to Thee when I am in trouble, how much
  more
  shall I turn to Thee when I am not in trouble!
To thank Thee for all my health, and for the prospect
  of brighter days ahead;
To ask Thee for the good sense to enjoy my health,
  but not to waste it.
To offer Thee my body, my will, my mind.

Shut up in this little room, surrounded by these four bare walls, keep me, O Lord, from feeling cut off from life. Let the air I breathe and the light I see be the signs to me of the Life that comes in from outside. Let the kindness that surrounds me and the care that never lets me go be the center of a world too big to ever cramp me and too good to blot me out.

Submitted by
The Rev. Richard T. Loring, Rector
Saint Luke's Church
Chelsea, Massachusetts

The Happier Periods Of Our Lives

Our Heavenly Father,
We thank you for the privilege of being able to meet as
a group of caring people. You have chosen us to be sur-
vivors, and may we appreciate that gift.

May we be thankful for the happier periods of our lives
when our loved ones were with us. As we care and share,
open our eyes to see the needs of others; teach our ears
to listen; keep our arms ever outstretched; and may our
mouths warmly express our loving concerns.

We must always realize that putting our problems, our
heartaches, and our lives into your care is so rewarding.
To some of us it is the key for progressing through grief
more quickly.

Bless each one here and may this evening be helpful to
all. This I ask in Jesus' name.

Amen.

Jean Knowles
Christ Presbyterian Church
Edina, MN

Thy Pain Put To Flight

I anoint thee with oil (or I lay my hand upon thee) . . . in the name of the Father, and of the Son, and of the Holy Ghost, beseeching the mercy of our Lord Jesus Christ, that all thy pain and sickness of body being put to flight, the blessing of health may be restored unto thee.

Amen.

Submitted by *Kay Moore*
Episcopalian
Red Hook, New York
From Book of Common Prayer, 1929.

Thanks For Springtime

Kind and Loving Father,

We thank thee for springtime, the green grass, flowers, singing birds, tiny lacy leaves on the trees, and more especially that we can enjoy them all. The world seems so much more beautiful at this season of the year. May we capture that feeling of change in our lives.

As we meet in your house, may we be able to care and share each others heartaches, problems, and questions. In love, some personal concerns are being shared, but others are known only to you.

You are a loving God. Help us come close to you, to trust you, and to put our faith in you. When we give you our problems, we find our pains dim, our problems seem more solvable, and our little world looks brighter. I know — because I have made that choice.

Bless our leader as she guides us and our member who will share her witness with us. Bless each one here this evening. When we leave, let us feel uplifted by your healing spirit. May we walk with you as we need thee every hour.

In your Son's name,
Amen

Jean Knowles
Christ Presbyterian Church
Edina, MN

Blessed Are You, Lord Our God
Whose Messenger Is Death . . .

Lord and Conductor of the Universe, we acknowledge and affirm the mystery of sunsets and farewells, of departures and finales as integral notes in your divine chorus.

We are thankful even for the pains of daily dying, for the daily separations that are the counterpoint in our common lives.

With gratitude we listen to the yearly song of creation, the melody of spring, summer and autumn which rises till the death-rest of winter, only to begin again in the resurrection of spring.

We take joy as our hearts rise to You, that this divine harmony of death and life was sung by prophets and holy people, and that your son, Jesus, sang that song with His whole person in His death and resurrection from the tomb.

We are grateful for His living example, for Him who found it so difficult departing from His friends so that a greater experience of life might be His and theirs.

In His footsteps, along that path of death and resurrection, we process toward our own death and resurrection in You.

Help us, Compassionate God, to let Your ancient and eternal song of death and life be played out in each of us, as we live out our faith that death is but a doorway that opens unto a greater and fuller expression of life, that opens to a final union with You who *are* life!

Blessed are You, Lord of Life, who alone knows the hour of our death and ultimate union with You.

Blessed are You, Lord our God, whose messenger is death.

Amen.

Submitted by *Dave Henton*
Austin, Texas
from *Prayers for the Domestic Church* by
Edward Hay.

For Trust In God

Oh God, the source of all health: so fill my heart with faith in your love that with calm expectancy I may make room for your power to possess me, and gracefully accept your healing. Through Jesus Christ, our Lord.

Amen

Rita Montenegro
Chicago, IL

You Are Our Hope

Dear Father,

May we realize that you are our hope, our provider and protector, our best friend, and that your love is unconditional and forever surrounds us.

Jean Knowles
Christ Presbyterian Church
Edina, MN

BOOK EIGHT

My Prayer

Lord, help me live from day to day
In such an humble sort of way,
To give a smile, help lift a load
For those I meet along life's road.
And when I come to my journey's end,
My life I have not lived in vain,
If one dear friend can smile and say
I'm glad I met her on life's way.

Anonymous

Mary E. Rich
Louisville, Kentucky

Watch Thou, Dear Lord

Watch Thou, Dear Lord, with those who wake, or over those who sleep, or weep tonight, and give Thine angels charge over those who sleep. Tend Thy sick ones, O Lord Christ. Rest Thy weary ones. Bless Thy dying ones. Soothe Thy suffering ones. Pity Thine afflicted ones. Shield Thy joyous ones. And all, for Thy Love's sake.

Amen — St. Augustine

Leonie Miller, Vice Governor
International Order of St. Luke the Physician
Tampa, Florida

Patience

God, please give me patience. The doctors do not yet know what is causing my distress. They are making many tests. Over and again, they have taken samples of my blood. They have probed me, listened to my heart, x-rayed me, injected me. And I wait—and wait—and wait! It is very hard to wait hours, even days, for results. I am anxious and sometimes frightened. But, the laboratory technicians and the doctors cannot hurry the process. Every test must be carefully done and evaluated. Why look for the worst and not consider the best? Oh, Lord, please help me to stop worrying—that I may use this time for reflection and to count my blessings.

Taken from the "Dear Abby" column by Abigail Van Buren. Copyright 1987. Universal Press Syndicate. Reprinted with permission. All rights reserved. Original by Rabbi Bernard Raskas, Temple of Aaron, St. Paul, MN

How Do I Visualize God?

Is he a Superstar, a Machoman who always has His
   way?
Whose tremendous resources could overwhelm and
   destroy
   an unfavored one in seconds?
Someone so powerful that He created the world
   and everything in it in just a few days—
   and could destroy it in a moment?

But that is not my God—
   one to fear solely from quaking terror
   one to hide from because of His wrath.

My God is a forgiving Deity
   a person who created me in His image.
A power who loves me with such a consuming love
   that He forgives.

He can pick me up in His hand and nurse me back
   to health,
   which he does.
He can create an invisible shield of protection around
   me
   to keep away evil things.
He can restoreth my soul, which He does.

I know that He has not forgotten me.
He knows of my illness and helps me.

He directs me down the road I am to take
  and whatever that road
I know it will be best for me.

I know there is nothing without Him.
  Without Him, there is no past.
  Without Him, there is no present.
  Without Him, there is no future.

I sleep, in the knowledge that He plans my future,
  knowing it's better in His hands
  than in those of a mortal like me.

My final thought is to beseech the Lord
  to be with me always
  to reveal His presence
  and to direct my actions.

In the name of His beloved Son, Jesus the Christ, I say
  these things.

Amen.

William H. Hull
Minneapolis, MN

While I Can

Oh, my Father, in Heaven, hear this, my humble plea. It is no small thing that troubles me, for my heart is heavy with the knowledge of men's words that say . . . "It's only a matter of time."

Whether I be in Christ or not in Christ, this knowledge, who can bear alone? I know there are my friends and family who share this burden, but it only grieves me more to see them so troubled. For these, I wish only happiness and health . . . all the days of their lives. But they grieve with me.

Therefor, O Lord, I pray . . . first of all that, my prayers will be heard. Secondly, I pray for mercy for any wrongs that I have committed against thee or my fellow man . . . and thirdly, I pray for healing. Not the mere healing of the body is what I ask for . . . but even more so, the healing of the soul, the spirit and the mind. For when these things work together they make me strong. If God be for me, and give me strength, then who can stand against me?

Thus, my healing will be complete. Even so, I know that all men must die, and in due time, I must render up this breath of life. Death comes to all . . . but life comes but to a few. So then . . . let me love life and let me live it to the fullest while I am able. For the fullness of life is found in Christ and death reigns as king where Christ does not.

While I can speak . . . let me say words of joy, hope and encouragement.

While I can touch . . . let me reach out to others in love and compassion.

And while I can see . . . let me see God in my fellow man.

And while I can reason . . . let me pray . . . not only for myself but for others . . . for these might return the blessing . . . when I cannot.

And while I can hear . . . let me hear wisdom and let me hear you. Let me hear the voices of those that I love . . . and those I want yet to love.

For this I pray . . . in Jesus name and for his name's sake.

Amen.

Rita R. Trafford
Lebanon, Indiana

Totally

I am totally disappointed . . . and my faith is almost gone.
Still . . . something deep inside me insists "You
must go on".
Totally devastated . . . by this loss . . . I see no
gain.
No purpose in my suffering . . . no healing in my
pain.

Totally surrounded . . . I must conclude at
last . . .
A shadow on my future . . . this calamity has cast.
I am totally destroyed . . . the walls have fallen
down.
All the precious things are taken . . . The King has
lost his crown.

I am totally forsaken . . . in what appears an end-
less grief.
It's so hard for my bleeding heart to muster up
belief.
Yet totally my spirit cannot admit defeat . . .
And will not lie upon its back . . . but struggles to
its feet.

Its eyes look up toward heaven and its voice is heard
to say,
"Why hast thou forsaken me?" and it begins to pray.

A "war" within . . . of fear and doubt . . . who'll
    win? . . . I cannot say,
But my spirit and my being both begin to pray.

For the heart, it beats, and the body breathes . . . The
    eyes still look to see . . .
The voice cries . . . and the world denies . . . but
    yet I am not free
For in this hell where men may dwell I know that God
    must be . . .
A "total God" is there somewhere and I believe it
    "Totally".

Rita R. Trafford
Lebanon, Indiana

INDEX OF AUTHORS
AND PRAYERS